# A
# HISTORY
# OF *Art*

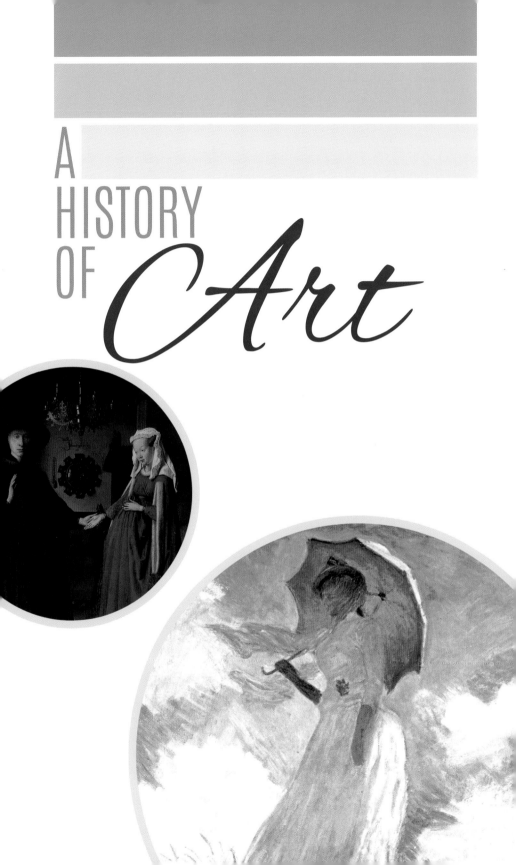

ESSENTIAL LIBRARY OF CULTURAL HISTORY

# A HISTORY OF *Art*

by Laura Perdew

**Content Consultant**
Dr. Charles Lachman
Associate Professor
History of Art and Architecture
University of Oregon

An Imprint of Abdo Publishing | www.abdopublishing.com

**www.abdopublishing.com**

Published by Abdo Publishing, a division of ABDO, PO Box 398166, Minneapolis, Minnesota 55439. Copyright © 2015 by Abdo Consulting Group, Inc. International copyrights reserved in all countries. No part of this book may be reproduced in any form without written permission from the publisher. Essential Library™ is a trademark and logo of Abdo Publishing.

Printed in the United States of America, North Mankato, Minnesota
102014
012015

Cover Photos: Everett Collection/Shutterstock Images
Interior Photos: Public Domain, 1 (left), 1 (right), 3 (top), 40, 42, 45, 50, 59, 61, 65, 100; Diane Bondareff/AP Images, 3 (bottom), 11; Keystone, Georgios Kefalas/AP Images, 7; Musee Marmottan Monet, Paris/Glow Images, 13; Christian Kober 1/Alamy, 15; CM Dixon/Glow Images, 17; iStock/Thinkstock, 23, 25, 32, 98, 99; PHB.cz/Richard Semik/ Shutterstock Images, 30; Yvan Travert/PhotoNonStop/Glow Images, 31; Bargello National Museum, Florence, Italy/Glow Images, 35; Red Line Editorial, 44; Jose Ignacio Soto/ Shutterstock Images, 47; Metropolitan Museum of Art/Boltin Picture Library/Bridgeman Images, 55; SuperStock/Glow Images, 56; Shutterstock Images, 67, 89, 97; Private Collection/Glow Images, 69; Hermitage, St. Petersburg, Russia/Bridgeman Images, 71; Art Institute of Chicago, Illinois, USA/Superstock/Glow Images, 77; The Phillips Collection, Washington, D.C., USA/Bridgeman Images, 79; Alastair Grant/AP Images, 81, 101; Heritage Images/Glow Images; 85; © Bridget Riley 2014. All rights reserved, courtesy Karsten Schubert, London/Bridgeman Art, 86; Maurizio Biso/Shutterstock Images, 91

Editor: Blythe Hurley
Series Designer: Maggie Villaume

**Library of Congress Control Number: 2014943858**

**Cataloging-in-Publication Data**

Perdew, Laura.
 A history of art / Laura Perdew.
  p. cm. -- (Essential library of cultural history)
 ISBN 978-1-62403-551-7 (lib. bdg.)
 Includes bibliographical references and index.
 1. Art--History--Juvenile literature.   I. Title.
 709--dc23

                                        2014943858

# CONTENTS

# Chapter 1

# What Is Art?

*M*ost people would say that they recognize art when they see it. But what is art, really? What do we mean when we say the word *art*? Are intricately balanced rocks in a creek a form of art? How about splattered paint on a canvas? Or a carved column on an ancient building? What about a stick figure drawn with crayon?

Most people think of art as something beautiful and creative that expresses important ideas or feelings. But what an individual sees as beautiful depends on his or her culture, values, and experiences. Art historians believe beauty is not simply a colorful image or a smooth marble statue. They believe the power of a work of art comes from its ability to evoke emotion or insight.

People throughout history have created and valued art for many different reasons. But what is art, really?

## MEDIA

In art, the term *media* refers to the materials an artist uses to create a piece. The oldest human art forms were carved from stone, shaped from clay, or painted on rock walls. Humans later sculpted works of art from marble, wood, ivory, and other materials. Today's sculptors use a wide variety of media, from plastics to steel. Prehistoric peoples used animal, plant, and mineral materials to make their paints. Painters today use oil paint, acrylics, and watercolors. New, modern media also include digital photography, video, and computer-generated art.

Must a work be created by an artist to be considered art? If so, what makes someone an artist? For a long time after the invention of the camera, photographers were not considered artists. Photos were not seen as a form of art but rather as a mechanical process. Today, few people would say photography is not art.

Likewise, for thousands of years, women were not considered artists in the male-dominated world. Those women who did participate in the arts were often not taken seriously. Others had their work attributed to male artists or simply left their work unsigned. In the Western world of today, however, the artistic abilities of women are considered every bit as worthwhile as those of their male counterparts.

French-American artist Marcel Duchamp's work in the early twentieth century is famous for raising questions about what art is and what it means to be an artist. One of his most famous works is an embellished recreation of Leonardo da Vinci's well-known *Mona Lisa* painting. Duchamp's piece is a fraction of the size of the original, and includes a mustache and beard on the figure. Duchamp intended to ridicule the world's fascination with *Mona Lisa* and reverence for oil paintings. His piece suggests anything can be art, so long as it is seen as such.

American pop artist Andy Warhol also addressed the question of what art is. He suggested art is not about skill or beauty at all. Instead, it is about communicating an idea. He believed art is a visual language. Therefore, the quality of a work should be judged not on the technical ability used to create the piece. Instead, it should be judged on the power of the message it broadcasts.

## Looking at Art

One does not need to be an art historian or even an artist to look at and enjoy art. In museums, people are attracted to certain pieces for many different reasons. Perhaps one of the best ways to think about art is to consider one's personal response to a piece and why it may or may not be attractive or interesting. Viewers might also think about the title of the work, the artist's life, and the time period in which the piece was created. Viewers can also consider how a work of art is composed, the lines and shapes it presents, and its patterns, textures, and colors.

# Context

Ultimately, art is subjective, both for the creator and the audience. When artists create their work, they are interpreting the world as they see it or portraying their feelings or the unconscious. Those who view art are likewise seeing it from their own perspective. Our own personal histories and experiences shape what we see. Thus, in order to understand the message a work of art is trying to share, one must be aware of an artist's background and his or her place in history.

In 1999, for example, the Brooklyn Museum showed an exhibition that included a piece titled *The Holy Virgin Mary* by British artist Chris Ofili. Far from the religious oil paintings of the Middle Ages, Ofili's piece depicted a black Virgin Mary using several different media including paint, glitter, and collage. The picture was not hung on the wall, but sat on two mounds of dried elephant dung. The work was met with both admiration and outrage. To many, the piece was offensive. However, the artist meant the picture to portray the holiness of the Virgin. Further, the elephant dung, which angered so many people, is actually sacred in Zimbabwe.

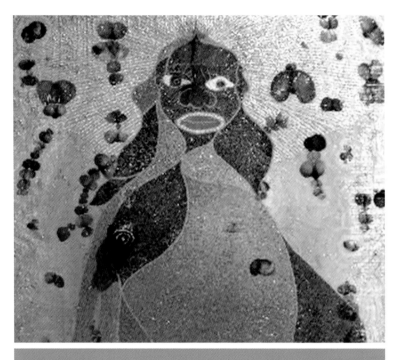

Chris Ofili's painting *The Holy Virgin Mary* sparked controversy when it was first displayed, yet many of its critics misunderstood the context of the author's message.

Likewise, what is considered art is always in flux. It varies from culture to culture and time period to time period. Even within a single culture at the same time, people disagree about what should be considered art. When Claude Monet first exhibited *Impression: Sunrise* (1872) at a show in 1874, critics hated it. Monet's piece was so different from the naturalistic work of Western artists of the time people did not consider it a true work of art. Yet today, critics consider Monet one of the leading artists of all time. Throughout history, those who have dared to move beyond the confines of what is considered art in their time period were often met with contempt. Yet these are the same artists who propelled art in new directions, who began new art movements, and who fill the pages of art history textbooks. Art, therefore, is the human imagination in action. It is the artist's expression of ideas and feelings, reflecting the world through his or her eyes at a specific period in time.

## Western Art Explored

The study of art is a journey into the history of human expression, experimentation, and imagination. The scope of art history spans the globe and traces the history of humankind to its origins. Western art has its roots in Europe. It includes the art of the United States, as the vast numbers of Europeans who migrated to the United States brought with them European influences.

The history of Western art can be told in stories of successive art movements, beginning with prehistoric art, continuing with the artwork of the Greek and Roman civilizations, and ending with the contemporary art of the 2000s. Art historians often dispute the

Claude Monet's *Impression: Sunrise* was hated by critics when it was first exhibited. But Monet went on to become one of the most important artists in history.

specific definitions and dates of these movements. But they do agree on general terms and dates defining these movements. These particulars, however, are not essential to understanding art. What is essential is the context in which a work of art was created. Who was the artist? What was that person's background? When and where was the work created? What was happening in the world at that time? One must always consider whose story is being revealed and from which perspective. One must also recognize there are many ways to interpret a piece of artwork.

# Chapter 2

# Caves, Carvings, and Classics

One day in 1879, a 12-year-old girl named Maria accompanied her father as he explored their property in Altamira, Spain. The father was looking for flint and animal bones. As they wandered, Maria spotted a small opening in the ground she hadn't seen before. She crawled through and discovered she was inside a cave chamber. The ceiling was decorated with pictures, including elaborate images of bison. Ultimately, experts determined these prehistoric cave paintings were more than 14,000 years old.

Similar remarkable discoveries have been made across Europe, some dating back to 30,000 BCE. These works were created around the time of the

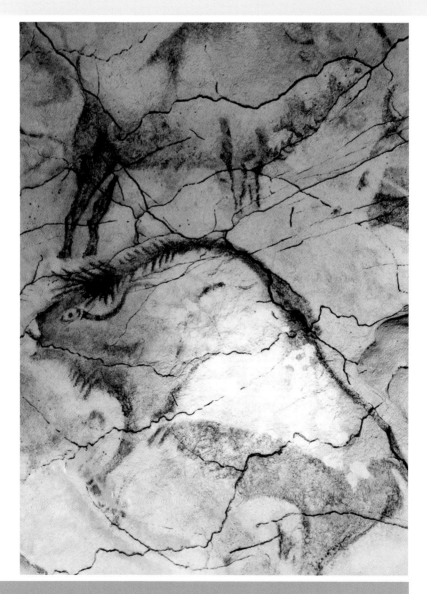

No one knows exactly why prehistoric humans created images such as this painting of bison discovered in Altamira, Spain.

Neanderthals, early humans who lived somewhere between 300,000 and 100,000 years ago. These pictures often depict animals such as the bison Maria found, horses, marine creature, cows, and more. Experts have debated the purpose of such images. One possibility is that these paintings were created simply to decorate the cave walls. Anthropologists in the 1900s dismissed that idea, however. They believed the cave paintings allowed prehistoric people to make sense of their world and to assert their place in it. Others believed the pictures told stories, creating a written history without words. Still others hold the cave paintings served some religious or ritualistic purpose for their creators. At the same time, many believe the pictures also seem to portray a reverence for animals and the hunt.

Sculptures have likewise been found that date back tens of thousands of years. Perhaps the most famous of these is the *Venus of Willendorf*, discovered in Austria in 1908 and created sometime between 28,000 and

Experts believe the famous *Venus of Willendorf* statue to be more than 25,000 years old, making it one of the earliest known depictions of the human figure.

25,000 BCE. Carved out of limestone, this small figurine stands only 4 3/8 inches (11 cm) tall.[1] Experts believe it to be more than 25,000 years old. It is named

Venus after the Roman goddess of love. Like many other Venus figures, this sculpture portrays the female form in an abstract way, accentuating her rounded breasts and swollen stomach while minimizing her arms and facial features. Archaeologists debate the meaning of this and similar figurines, but suggest their existence may show their creators' respect for women as child bearers.

While no one is sure of the purpose behind these ancient paintings and sculptures, their existence nonetheless shows very early humans had an awareness of themselves and the world around them. At some point tens of thousands of years ago, people evolved beyond acting simply on the instinct for survival to become conscious, creative individuals. These paintings and objects give evidence for the birth of art.

## Stonehenge

In the south of England stands one of humankind's most famous architectural creations. Stonehenge, created sometime between 2750 and 1300 BCE, is one of many structures erected using massive stones. The 24-foot- (7.3 m) tall rough-cut stones are arranged vertically in two concentric rings.[2] Each pair of stones supports another massive stone block placed horizontally on top. This style of construction, using a "post" (the vertical stone) supporting a "lintel" (the horizontal stone), is still used today. The outer ring of stones is arranged to align with the sun's trajectory at the summer solstice, though historians still do not know why these stones were moved here from afar and arranged this way.

# The Roots of the Western Tradition

Over time, humans developed more complex societies, systems of authority, and art. One of the greatest civilizations to emerge in the ancient Western world was that of Greece, beginning around 900 BCE. It was here Western art is believed to have begun.

Greek art was dominated by sculpture, generally human figures. The work of Greek artists called attention to the beauty of the human figure. Even gods and goddesses were portrayed in human form. These sculptures also reveal that the Greeks studied the human body in great detail, and attempted to portray it realistically. One famous work, *Kritios Boy* (created sometime around 480 BCE), serves as a primary example of Greek sculpture. The figure is almost three feet tall (0.9 m), and is carved from marble.[3] This statue reveals much about the advancements of Greek art. The artist who sculpted *Kritios Boy* was one of the first to show how people really stand. The boy has his weight shifted onto his left leg, with his right leg bent. His head is also slightly tilted, whereas most previous statues stood stiff-legged, looking straight ahead.

Long periods of prosperity and stability allowed the Greeks to undertake great building projects as well. Initially influenced by earlier Egyptian and Mesopotamian buildings, Greek architects soon developed their own style. They experimented with column design and use, the distribution of the weight of the stone they used, and visual effects created by their massive buildings.

The hilltop complex known as the Acropolis was constructed at the height of Greek civilization. Within its citadel is the structure known as the Parthenon, built sometime around 440 BCE. It is a temple to Athena, the goddess of wisdom. It was designed using mathematical precision, symmetry, and balance and is part sculpture, part architecture. With eight columns across its front and back and seventeen on each side, this structure has become a symbol of classical Greek architecture.

## Roman Civilization

The Roman Empire, one of the greatest civilizations in history, began around 750 BCE and peaked between 27 BCE and 337 CE. The artists of the Roman Empire were heavily influenced by Grecian styles. Yet the Romans borrowed these ideas and used them to create something new that reflected their own efficiency and organization.

As with the Greeks, once the Roman culture established stability and dominance, grand building projects were undertaken throughout the empire. One of the purposes of these projects was to reinforce Roman authority among the people. Much of the success and progress of Roman architecture was due to the development of concrete. Not only was this material strong and inexpensive but it also allowed builders to mold its shape. The result was that Roman architecture was free to explore new forms that had previously been impossible. These structures became a trademark of Roman-style architecture.

One example is the Pantheon, "the temple of all gods," built between 118 and 28 CE. The front is adorned with eight massive columns,

## GREEK AND ROMAN ARCHITECTURE IN WASHINGTON, DC

A true testament to the dominance and sophistication of classical Greek and Roman culture lies in the fact that classical styles of architecture still thrive throughout the world today. Many of the architects and designers who created government buildings and monuments in the capital of the United States turned to the Greek and Roman cultures for architectural inspiration. The Lincoln Memorial, for example, was built in the style of a Greek temple. The influence of the Roman Pantheon can be seen in the design of the National Museum of Natural History. Union Station, the Capitol building, the Jefferson Memorial, and many other important buildings stand as examples of the legacy of Greek and Roman architecture.

in keeping with Greek tradition. But the inside is fully Roman. Just behind the front columns is an immense dome, 142 feet (43.3 m) wide, with a 27-foot- (8.2 m) wide opening allowing light to enter the interior.[4] The distance from the floor to the peak of the dome measures 142 feet (43.3 m).[5] This creates a vast, open interior space that is even grander than the exterior. It was this fusion of traditional architecture with innovative design that allowed the construction of such a massive dome. This building still stands as one of Roman culture's greatest achievements.

Detailed wall paintings were another common feature of Roman art. They often featured realistic representations of specific individuals in portrait form. Other styles sought to create the illusion that the walls were actually made of expensive marble, just as modern decorators today use less-costly materials to

## Pompeii's Contribution to Western Art

When Mount Vesuvius erupted in 79 CE, it was a catastrophe for the city of Pompeii. Located near the Bay of Naples in the Roman Empire, the volcano had been dormant for a long time. Its eruption caught people off guard, and many were killed instantly. The result, however, was a well-preserved snapshot of life and art in that period. The city's wall paintings reveal the skill of Roman painters was quite advanced at that time. The artists' work shows their understanding of depth and the ability to portray the elements of a story.

The fresco paintings of the buried city of Pompeii preserve Roman art from the first century CE.

imitate expensive ones. Realistic paintings created the illusion of a three-dimensional picture. Artists painted murals depicting windows, gates, or doors to create the sense that the room extended beyond its walls to a garden, courtyard, or village.

The influence of ancient Greek and Roman art extended far beyond their civilizations. Artists and architects throughout history have embraced the classical styles of ancient Greece and Rome, which stress balance, perfection, order, and beauty.

# Chapter 3

# The Middle Ages

The Middle Ages refers to the time period between the fall of the Roman Empire and the period known as the Renaissance. The Middle Ages is also sometimes called the medieval time period. This era encompasses approximately 1,000 years of history, from 400 to 1400 CE. During this time, Christianity spread and became the dominant religion across Europe.

The subject of medieval art was almost universally religion. Closely aligned with political authorities, religious institutions commissioned medieval artists to create artwork that glorified God. Art's purpose, especially for mosaics and paintings, was also to educate and convert the masses. Artists used figures and

The elaborate design of Old Saint Peter's Basilica in Rome, Italy, forever influenced church architecture in Western Europe.

symbols to tell the story of Christianity and explain the foundations of the Christian faith. Their works merged styles from across Europe. The result was artwork full of figurative images that communicated religious stories yet was also ornately decorative.

## Churches

Churches and cathedrals were built across Europe after Emperor Constantine declared Christianity the official religion of the Roman Empire in 313. Artists designed grand churches featuring high vaults and large windows with the idea of creating dwellings suitable for God and the saints on Earth. The designs maximized the play of natural light on stained glass, mural paintings, gold adornments, crosses, and candlesticks in an attempt to imitate biblical tales of paradise on Earth.

## Jewish Art

Throughout the Middle Ages, Jews were a minority in Europe and faced constant persecution. Despite this, the Jewish community made great contributions to medieval European culture, including the arts. Jewish synagogues, decorated with mural paintings, display the skill of Jewish artists working in the Roman tradition. One of the best surviving examples is the Dura-Europos synagogue in present-day Syria. Built in the third century, this synagogue is adorned with wall murals, painted ceilings, and other decorations. Similar to Christian artworks that depict biblical stories, these murals illustrate events from Hebrew holy texts.

Old Saint Peter's Basilica in Rome was one of the first of these grand structures to be built. Designed in the Roman tradition, it featured a long, rectangular hall and two side aisles. The entry courtyard, called the atrium, led to a porch and the church's doorways. Commissioned by Emperor Constantine, the church was completed around 329. Its basilica-style design forever influenced church architecture in Western Europe.

Old Saint Peter's Basilica could hold as many as 14,000 worshipers.[2]

The Byzantine church Hagia Sophia was erected in what is now Turkey between 532 and 537. The dome of the church was the largest in the world at the time, and the entire structure is more than 40 feet (12 m) higher than the Pantheon in Rome.[1] The building's architects wanted to use light as a metaphor for wisdom. To create this spiritual quality, they designed the dome to sit on 40 windows, producing a halo of light in the interior of the structure. The inside of Hagia Sophia is richly decorated with colored stones. The use of traditional Greek and Roman architecture, combined with Asian influences, changed the course of architecture. The

Hagia Sophia is still considered one of the world's greatest architectural achievements.

Church construction continued through the Middle Ages, culminating in the Age of the Great Cathedrals from approximately 1150 to 1250. During this time, Gothic-style art and architecture evolved, lasting into the 1500s. This new approach is known for its grandeur and richness. Leaders throughout Europe attempted to make their churches larger and more lavish than those built before. Architects at the time used rib vaults, flying buttresses, and pointed arches in order to build increasingly tall structures that could still be illuminated by natural light. One of the most famous examples of this type of architecture is the Cathedral of Notre Dame in Paris, France, constructed during the 1100s and 1200s.

## Decorating the Churches

While the cathedrals and churches built during the Middle Ages were themselves works of art, they were also adorned with paintings, mosaics, and stained glass. Much of the art produced during this time portrayed the narratives of the Bible. Church leaders commissioned these works in order to teach people about the life and message of Jesus Christ. In addition, the paintings sought to evoke emotion and force introspection. Artists painted murals on the walls, ceilings, and catacombs of many of the great cathedrals and churches.

Mosaics also served both to adorn the massive walls of the great new churches and to depict biblical stories. Early Christian artists transformed the Roman art of mosaics by using colored glass shards. This allowed for a much wider array of color and created beautiful displays when the shards reflected the light that filtered into the churches as a result of the newly developed architectural styles. Light poured in from above, dancing and reflecting off the individual glass pieces, creating the illusion that the walls glittered.

## Illuminated Manuscripts

Illuminated manuscripts were an important art form during the Middle Ages. Similar to paintings, the illustrations in these manuscripts portray biblical scenes in great detail and vivid color. In Gothic Europe, the city of Paris became renowned for its fine book production. While this art form originally fell under the command of the church, it evolved to become a realm in which professional artists sold their work to the public. The workshops of these artists are thought to be the predecessor of today's modern publishing houses.

# FLYING
## *Buttresses*

Gothic architecture was characterized by lavish design and decoration. But one of the less exciting visual features of these grand structures is also one of their most essential architectural elements. The protruding masonry arches known as flying buttresses are fundamental to these buildings' stability. This type of support was first introduced during the early 1100s. Originally large, clunky, and awkward, flying buttresses became far more delicate and ornate by the 1200s.

Saint Barbara's Cathedral, Kutna Hora, Czech Republic

*Flying Buttress*

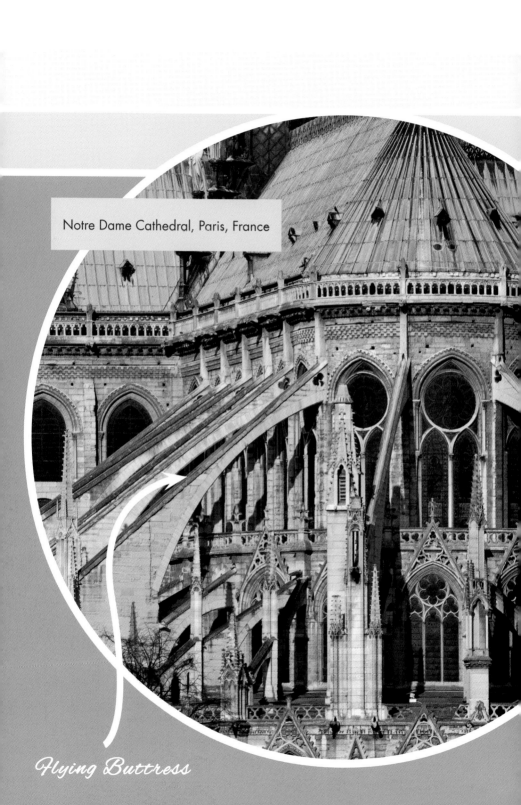

Notre Dame Cathedral, Paris, France

*Flying Buttress*

This thoughtful-looking gargoyle adorns the world-famous Notre Dame Cathedral in Paris, France.

Stained glass emerged as a major decorative art form during the Gothic era. As with paintings and mosaics, stained glass images represented sacred figures and events. But unlike other artistic decorations, stained glass was used to replace walls instead of to embellish them. The light that passes through these stained glass creations colors the interior of the churches and everyone in it. In addition, changing light conditions outside change the effects inside. This passage of light was meant to symbolize the Christian faith, representing the transmission of God into the hearts of worshipers.

By the end of the 1300s, things began changing. Scholars, intellectuals, and even ordinary citizens began questioning the unquestioned dominance of the church. They reexamined the remarkable accomplishments of the Greeks and Romans, and began focusing less on the church as the path to salvation and more on human achievement and exploring the natural world. This cultural shift marked the end of the Middle Ages.

## GARGOYLES

Stone carvings of beastly animals, grotesque faces, or monstrous creatures are often seen clinging to the outsides of medieval churches and cathedrals. These gargoyles have been thought to ward off evil spirits or to remind worshipers of the fate that awaits those who do not follow the path to salvation. In fact, however, gargoyles are also a part of the gutter systems of these buildings, diverting water away from cathedral walls. Some experts believe this practice has its roots in Greek and Roman architecture, which sometimes included animal-shaped water spouts used for drainage.

# Chapter 4

# The Rebirth of Classical Ideas

$\mathcal{B}$y the 1300s, many people had begun questioning the church's authority. At the same time, scholars took a fresh look at the art, science, and philosophy of classical Greece and Rome. Humanism, a philosophy that places value on people and their accomplishments as opposed to divine entities, began taking root as the church's authority weakened. This secular thinking also allowed for more scientific investigation, increased interest in the natural world, and advances in mathematics. In art, this period spawned a reexamination of Greek and Roman approaches to art and design and new styles inspired by them. It also meant artists had more freedom to explore nonreligious subject matter.

The artists of the Renaissance portrayed the human body accurately, as seen here in Donatello's sculpture *David*.

During the early part of the 1300s, the poet Petrarch recognized the cultural shift taking place. He described the era as "a revival of the classics." This time period, from roughly 1400 to 1600, came to be known as the Renaissance, which means "rebirth" in French.

## The Renaissance Takes Root

Although the cultural changes of the Renaissance spread across Europe, its epicenter is often considered to be Florence, in modern-day Italy. Unlike many other European cities at the end of the 1300s, Florence had a thriving economy and a progressive, stable political system. Around the same time, the Ottoman Empire conquered the city of Constantinople, and the dominating Christian Byzantine culture collapsed. This caused many of the city's scholars to migrate

## Giotto: Father of the Renaissance

During the 1300s, a famous painter met a young shepherd boy with artistic talent. The painter befriended the boy and taught him about painting. Eventually this boy, Giotto di Bondone, became a more accomplished artist than his teacher. A historian in the 1500s later credited Giotto with "setting art upon the path that may be called the true one, [for he] learned to draw accurately from life and thus put an end to the crude [medieval] manners."[1] Even then, almost a century before the noted beginning of the Renaissance, Giotto combined the classical Greek style with humanism and three-dimensional forms.

to Florence. They brought with them classical ideas that had been dormant in Europe during the medieval period.

Both in Florence and across Europe, economic changes began taking place that allowed the gradual emergence of a social middle class. Patrons of the arts were no longer limited to the aristocracy and the church. Professionals such as bankers, merchants, and lawyers began commissioning artwork as well, and these new customers inspired artists to explore new subject matter and styles. This included an interest in themes from classical Greek and Roman culture, including human anatomy, perspective, and proportion.

# The Human Body

Images of human nudes were not part of Western art during the Middle Ages because the body was associated with worldly pleasure, something the church preached against. During the Renaissance, however, this philosophy changed. Although people did not discard their religious beliefs, they did begin to see the human form as one of God's creations. In addition, human nudes were a very important aspect of classical Greek and Roman art, and the artists of the Renaissance sought to emulate the ideal forms of the classical artists from those times. Throughout the Renaissance, artists also began portraying the human body accurately, including flaws and emotions.

The works of Italian sculptor Donatello were among the first to demonstrate this philosophical shift. Perhaps his most famous piece is a life-sized bronze sculpture of the biblical hero David. Donatello's *David*, created sometime in the early to mid-1400s, borrowed from the classical tradition of the Greeks. As with many Greek sculptures,

## PRINTMAKING

Printmaking was another significant artistic development during the Renaissance. This new technique resulted in printed books, leading to greater literacy and the spread of humanist thinking. It also changed how images could be shared. With this new technology, artists could create multiple copies of their works. Initially, the most common form of printmaking was woodcuts. Artists carved an image onto a wood block. Next, ink was applied to the block, with the low points remaining uncolored. Finally, the block was pressed onto paper, transferring the inked image.

*David* is a tribute to heroism and righteousness. This statue represents the ideal, fit, nude male. Yet the piece also broke new ground at the time. Donatello portrayed the youth as sensuous and victorious. The figure also wears a childish hat and boots and carries a rock and a slingshot. He stands with one foot atop the severed head of his enemy.

The hero David was used as a subject again less than a century later by another great Italian artist, Michelangelo. This marble statue, completed in 1504, also borrowed from the classical ideal of a male nude. Yet in Michelangelo's *David*, the figure is pensive as opposed to triumphant, a warrior contemplating an upcoming battle. This statue came to symbolize the idea of right over might, and it is still considered one of

## Frescoes

The word *fresco* means "fresh" in Italian. In art, it refers to a technique of painting on the final layer of plaster on a wall before it dries. The colors of the paint are then absorbed into the surface of the wall. Though artists had used this technique for thousands of years prior to the Renaissance, it became very popular during that time. Renaissance artists frequently created frescoes on the walls and ceilings of chapels. In 1512, Michelangelo completed one of the most famous frescoes in the world, the ceiling of the Sistine Chapel in Rome. It took him four years to create.

Leonardo da Vinci's work explored a wide variety of subject matter, including inventions, religious themes, human anatomy, and portraits, including the *Mona Lisa*.

the greatest sculptures ever created depicting the ideal human form.

Renowned artist Leonardo da Vinci is best known for famous paintings such as the *Mona Lisa* (created between 1503 and 1506) and the *Last Supper* (created between 1495 and 1498). Yet he had many talents and was an inventor of many things. In addition to painting, he also applied his brilliant mind to detailed anatomical drawings. One of his best-known pieces is titled *The Vitruvian Man* (created in 1490), which applies mathematical proportions and geometric shapes to a diagram of an ideal male figure.

## Naturalism

Naturalism, depicting the natural world as it truly is, emerged as a cornerstone of artistic expression during the Renaissance. This style of work includes reflections on water, minute details of plants and animals, and even the steam from a person's breath on a cold day. The result is work that is quite lifelike.

In northern Europe, the painter Jan van Eyck became well known for his impeccable representations of nature in his work. Van Eyck studied his subjects carefully and captured even the smallest details of hair texture and glittering gems. His paintings were described as a mirror to the natural world. Van Eyck is also credited by some as being among the first artists to popularize the use of oil paint, which enabled artists to create more textures and effects. Before the Renaissance, artists used an egg-based paint that was opaque and dried quickly. This limited an artist's ability to blend colors and create detail. Working with oil paint, which uses an oil to

Jan van Eyck was among the first artists to make extensive use of oil paint, as in the *Arlofini Portrait.*

bind ground pigments instead of egg, gives artists new opportunities. Since this type of paint dries slowly, artists have more time to work and rework portions of a painting. Oil paint also allows artists to create works that mimic nuances and fluctuations in light and color that more accurately mirror the real world.

## Perspective

Another great legacy of the Renaissance was the development of the system of linear perspective. Advances in mathematics led to new ways of representing the three-dimensional world on a two-dimensional surface such as a canvas, wall, or paper. To realistically show depth, artists define a horizon and a central vanishing point, the point at which the eye can no longer see things in the distance because they are too far away. In addition, artists portray objects in the foreground of a scene as larger than objects in the distance. Throughout the Renaissance, artists such as Leonardo da Vinci continued to study and experiment with perspective. Through his sharp observations, da Vinci also became aware of the differences in how objects look close up versus far away. Da Vinci noted objects in the distance appear less vibrant in color. The farther away the object, the more neutral blue-gray it appears. Objects in the distance also become less clear than those in the foreground. His observations led to a new artistic approach known as atmospheric perspective.

Artists including Donatello, Michelangelo, van Eyck, da Vinci, and others changed the course of art and art history through their astute observations and experiments with subject and media. It was on this foundation other art movements emerged at the end of the Renaissance, moving away from classical ideals and taking off in new directions.

# LINEAR
## *Perspective*

## PICTURE PLANE

Vanishing Point

Orthogonal Lines

Horizon Line

Transversal Lines

Ground Line

Linear perspective is an artistic technique that creates the illusion of depth and distance, making objects on a two-dimensional surface such as a painting or mural appear three-dimensional. This technique begins with establishing a horizon line, which defines the farthest distance of the background, and a central vanishing point. The artist then draws what are called orthogonal lines from the bottom of the picture area, called the ground line, which defines the foreground

Leonardo da Vinci, *The Last Supper*

of the space. Once these basic elements have been put in place, the artist may add further elements to create a more complicated and realistic space. For example, horizontal lines, called transversals, can add detail to the image, enhancing the illusion that the image is three-dimensional. Linear perspective allows artists to link three-dimensional geometry with artistic representation in two dimensions.

# Chapter 5

# Moving Away from Classical Ideals

*P*olitical, religious, and social change spread through Europe during the centuries following the Renaissance. Countries were beginning to assert their individual identities and authority. People were questioning the abuses of power of the Catholic Church, and secular concerns grew in importance. The new middle class, which was both literate and financially stable, continued growing.

A class of artists emerged as well. Many artists studied and worked as apprentices under master artists in places called workshops. Families sometimes sent their children (mostly boys) as young as 12 to work as apprentices. Often this work, which included taking

Baroque art and architecture embraced ornate detail, as seen in the Cathedral of Santiago de Compostela in Spain.

care of the shop and running errands, had nothing to do with art at all. As young artists gained skills, however, they could learn directly from the master. Eventually, if they showed promise, they could assist the master on simpler aspects of a work of art. In the end, when apprentices were able to create work that was accepted as art by the artistic community, they became masters themselves.

Art academies also grew in popularity at this time. These schools had their roots in 300s BCE Greece, when the philosopher Plato taught a school called the Academia. Later, during the 1400s and 1500s, schools for teaching and studying art were established. These schools, known as academies, emphasized the study of classic works of art, copying famous works, appraisal by teachers, lectures, and exhibitions. This type of formal training dictated the course of Western art for centuries.

## Baroque

The baroque art movement that emerged during the 1600s was characterized by ornate detail. Whereas Renaissance artists were concerned with the precision and order of classical art, those of the baroque era

(1600–1750) embraced excitement, drama, and extravagant ornamentation.

One of the great artists to emerge during this time was Italian painter Michelangelo Merisi da Caravaggio. He was a man with a colorful and violent past who rejected the classical traditions of the Renaissance. Unlike the idealized naturalism of the Renaissance, which depicts images of the aristocracy and the beauty of the natural world, Caravaggio painted ordinary people in a new style of naturalism. He painted the world he knew, not an idealized one. Caravaggio is also known for his skillful use of light to portray spiritual subjects. His work was initially secular. But in 1599, he received his first church commission. From that point on, Caravaggio specialized in creating religious paintings for the church. One of his first was *The Calling of Saint Matthew*, completed around 1600. The painting portrays the moment

## ARTEMISIA GENTILESCHI

Artemisia Gentileschi was an accomplished painter during the baroque era in Rome. Despite her skill and the commissions she received from wealthy patrons, Gentileschi believed she was treated unfairly because of her gender. For example, one of her patrons once commissioned another artist to copy one of Gentileschi's paintings. She wrote, "If I were a man, I can't imagine it would have turned out this way."[1] Nonetheless, she became the first woman to be admitted to the Accademia del Disegno, "Academy of Drawing," in Florence.

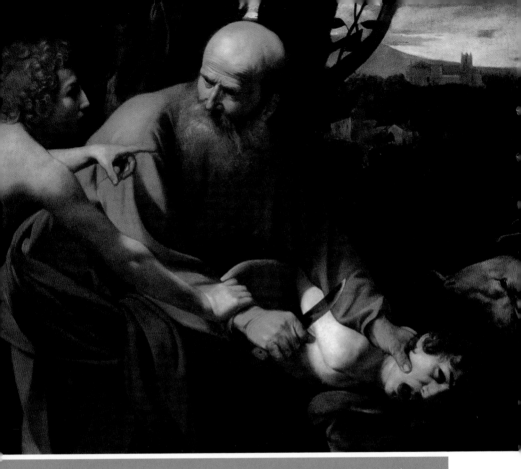

Italian painter Michelangelo Merisi da Caravaggio is known for his dramatic use of light and shadow, as seen in *The Sacrifice of Isaac.*

of the first meeting between Christ and Saint Matthew. But it does so in an entirely contemporary way, in both light and subject matter. Caravaggio's representation of a beam of light and shadow, which conveys the image's divine, spiritual content, is juxtaposed with the dark and mundane everyday world and everyday people. In addition, the image creates a dramatic narrative without words.

Among the sculptors of the baroque era, Gian Lorenzo Bernini emerged as one of the finest. In addition to his elaborate decoration in the new Saint Peter's Basilica and others across Rome, his work as a sculptor captured the spirit of the time. Critics have compared his sculpture *David* (1624) to those of Donatello and Michelangelo. While Donatello's *David* is sinuous and graceful, and Michelangelo's is a classical ideal human figure, Bernini's holds an offensive pose, ready to attack. His face is drawn and serious. The figure is very realistic.

As baroque art and architecture spread across Europe, King Louis XIV used art to communicate the glory and power of the monarchy in France. He became one of baroque art's greatest patrons. His grandest project was the Palace of Versailles. Like all baroque architecture, this structure is grandiose in size and decorated with lavish materials. The massive palace is more than one-quarter mile (0.4 km) long.[2] It includes a 240-foot (73 m) hall of mirrors that reflects the outside gardens and the sunlight.[3] The palace is richly decorated with wall paintings, chandeliers, and ornate furniture. The grounds include a landscaped park that extends from the palace for several miles. The palace, which was finished in 1685, took more than 15 years to construct.

In the Netherlands, baroque artists evolved even further to focus on portraits, still lifes, and landscapes from 1600 to 1700. One of the most influential and famous of these artists was Rembrandt Harmenszoon van Rijn. As a master artist, he not only taught his own students but also created detailed paintings, many with religious and symbolic themes. He is also known for his many portraits of himself and his contemporaries and for his use of light and shadow. Another great artist of the time was a woman, Judith Leyster. Her work was typical of the era, portraying lively, everyday scenes, as well as her now famous *Self-Portrait*, which she completed sometime around 1633. Not only was Leyster a talented painter, but she too had her own workshop and taught students. Yet as was typical of that era, she painted less and less after she was married. It wasn't until 1893 that her work, which had been attributed to another artist, was rediscovered.

# Romanticism

During the mid-1700s, European society changed in many ways. Political revolutions in France and the soon-to-be United States, as well as the Industrial Revolution, upended ways of life that had changed little for centuries. Romanticism emerged in Europe during the second half of the 1700s and lasted until approximately 1850. This movement celebrated freedom of emotion and thought. Among artists, this meant a focus on the imagination, evoking intense emotions, and turning away from the confines of classical art. More than ever before, artists attempted to create work that would evoke deeply moving, subjective experiences. Painters used soft, fluid brushstrokes, robust colors, and contrasts between light and dark to create dramatic compositions.

Nature was a common subject in romantic art. Paintings expressed the power, violence, and unpredictability of the natural world. This oftentimes included humanity's struggle against the power of nature, such as scenes showing shipwrecks or people overshadowed by the vastness of the Alps. Other works

## WATERCOLORS

The use of watercolor paints dates back to ancient civilizations. It is made by mixing a pigment with water and a binding agent, such as a gum or egg yolk. The paint is then thinned with water before being applied to a surface. Watercolors gained popularity in Europe during the 1700s and 1800s. Many artists interested in working outdoors choose watercolors because the paint is easily transportable, allowing artists to capture the colors of light and weather.

simply depict people's attitude toward nature and the emotions it evokes. A typical example of such work, *Evening: Landscape with an Aqueduct* (1818), is part of a series created by artist Théodore Gericault. It depicts a landscape at different times of day.

## Across the Pond

On the other side of the Atlantic Ocean, the United States was still a young country. Most American artists studied in Europe and emulated European movements of the time. It was not until approximately 1850 that the first distinct art movement in the United States emerged, the Hudson River school. The artists of this style studied and painted the distinct landscapes of the Hudson River Valley and the rest of New England.

One of the key figures of the group was Thomas Cole. Like other American landscape artists, he wanted to illustrate what made the country unique. Cole also used his work to underscore

Between 1804 and 1817, Thomas Jefferson designed the University of Virginia campus in Charlottesville, Virginia, in the classical Greek and Roman style.

American landscape artist Thomas Cole used his work, including *The Oxbow*, to explore ideas surrounding the development of the American wilderness.

the debate surrounding the development of the United States. In his 1836 oil painting *The Oxbow*, a natural plain with plowed fields and settlements is set against an ominous wilderness. The painting exposes a major question facing the United States at the time: how to balance an environmentally friendly agrarian society with the industrial development in urban areas.

## Realism

During the mid-1800s, advances in science led people to shift away from their focus on the feelings and emotions of the romantic era. Instead, people turned to scientific

studies as a way to understand human behavior, society, and the natural world.

Similar to Caravaggio during the baroque era, followers of the realist movement (from approximately 1840 to 1900) believed artists should find their subjects in the modern world in which they lived. Nothing was embellished or idealized. The work of this time depicted real people going about their everyday lives and the events of the second half of the nineteenth century. These included the grim realities of urban life, the hardships of peasant life, and the rapid changes occurring in Western society. Artists such as Gustave Courbet focused on representing the actual world and all of its realities. They also began to synthesize many different painting styles, beginning to change the way in which artists thought of painting in general and laying the groundwork for future art movements.

## JOHN JAMES AUDUBON

The realist painters of the 1800s had an important role in documenting the natural world prior to the invention of the camera. In the United States, watercolor painter John James Audubon set out to record the birds of America. He traveled extensively, making 435 watercolor paintings of birds using close observation. His illustrations revealed details about the birds and their habitats. In 1839, he published his work in an encyclopedia, *Birds of America*.

The meticulous illustrations created by John James Audubon preserved images of wildlife before the advent of the camera.

# Chapter 6

# Impressionism and Beyond

Until the middle of the 1800s, academic art dominated the art scene. Art was taught by established art schools and promoted through exhibitions, which in France were called *salons*. Academic works focused on traditional subjects and techniques rooted in the Renaissance. Yet some artists had begun exploring different forms of artistic expression.

These artists were regularly rejected entry into the salons because their work greatly departed from the standards of the day. In response to these rejections, a group of artists staged their own shows in Paris. The impressionist exhibitions took place every one or two years between 1874 and 1886.

Impressionist artists such as Claude Monet revolutionized art with works such as *Woman with a Parasol*, created in 1886.

The word *impressionist* was actually derived from the first of these shows, held in 1874, when Claude Monet exhibited a painting titled *Impression, Sunrise* (1872). The painting was quite different from the naturalistic, measured work Western artists had previously created. Instead, the piece appears two-dimensional and highlights the light and color of a sunrise over a body of water. Critics met Monet's work and that of others in the show with contempt. Referencing the title of Monet's painting, one critic called the whole exhibition "impressionist," which he meant as an insult. However, the artists happily adopted this term as the name of their movement because it reflected their intent to capture one moment's impression of a scene using spots of color to simulate the effects of different kinds of light.

## Everyday Life

Art historians often credit Monet with beginning the impressionism artistic movement. He ignored the rules artists were supposed to follow. He met regularly at a Paris café with other artists such as Pierre-Auguste Renoir, Paul Cézanne, and others. This is the same group of artists who exhibited together beginning in 1874 after being rejected by the salons. They shared Monet's desire to explore new boundaries in art.

Building on the idea of realism that had been established earlier in the century, impressionist artists used their works to try to capture a moment in time. Renoir's paintings explored the joys of life and

As shown in Pierre-Auguste Renoir's *Luncheon of the Boating Party,* impressionist artists used their works to try to capture realistic moments in time.

leisure activities. He created scenes from dance halls, concerts, the opera, and more. With his use of light and color, his paintings evoke the festive atmosphere of everyday scenes dappled in sunlight, as in his painting *Luncheon of the Boating Party* (1881). He created slightly blurred figures by using feathery brushstrokes, which results in a work that seems fleeting and momentary. American artist Mary Cassatt also exhibited with the impressionists, though she could not spend time at the cafés with the male artists because the etiquette of the era did not allow it. Her work portrays scenes of a woman's domain at the time. This focus on domestic scenes was a means for Cassatt to elevate the importance of women in society.

## EN PLEIN AIR

It is not surprising that most impressionists, who were so enamored by the play between light and color, preferred to work outdoors. Just as their work was a departure from tradition, so too was this choice to work *en plein air*, "in the open air." Impressionists such as Monet did much of their work outside in order to capture the moment, yet oftentimes returned to a studio to polish a piece. It is a style still employed by many contemporary artists.

## Light and Color

One of the keys to the impressionist movement was experimentation with light and color on the canvas. To this end, light actually became a subject for some painters. Artists sought to capture the effects of natural light on subjects and the colors developing from the light. Monet explained to a fellow artist, "When you go out to paint, try to forget what objects you have before you—a tree, a house, a field, or whatever. Merely think, here is a little square of blue, here an oblong of pink, here a streak of yellow, and paint it just as it looks to you, the exact color and shape, until it gives your own naïve impression of the scene before you."[1]

This means of depicting a scene also changed how people saw art. Traditionally, art was meant to be like looking through a window to the world. But impressionist artists weren't merely portraying a landscape. Instead, they were depicting the sensation produced by the landscape at a single moment in time.

## Pointillism

Just as the impressionists experimented with color, so too did Georges Seurat. But unlike the others, Seurat used thousands of dots. This practice of using dots of color to create an image is called pointillism. This technique experimented with emerging theories about color. One theory asserted that the eye perceives colors differently depending on the colors around it. Further, the eye tends to "mix" complementary colors as it perceives them. Seurat produced masterful works such as A Sunday on La Grande Jatte (completed in 1886) comprised solely of tiny dots.

# Postimpressionists

One of the legacies of the impressionist movement is that artists were becoming more free of the expectations of the academies and salons. This allowed them to pursue their own forms of artistic expression. Many artists began exploring new techniques during the impressionist era. In the 1880s and 1890s, artists such as Cézanne, Paul Gauguin, Vincent van Gogh, and others turned away from the impressionists' focus on capturing the light and color of a single moment. They returned to a more scholarly approach to art that was more structured. Their styles varied, but collectively, their work represented a new era of abstract styles full of feeling and symbolism.

Even though he only sold one painting during his lifetime, Van Gogh has become the most well-known representative of the postimpressionist movement.

## FAUVISM

Though short lived, the fauve movement in the early 1900s took the expressive use of color employed by the impressionists and postimpressionists to a completely new level. In fauvism, color became the single element for conveying meaning, as well as the force that holds a picture together. Henri Matisse was the unofficial leader of this movement, as his work used both bold and often nonrealistic coloring. Outraged by the "orgy of pure colors" in the work of Matisse and his colleagues, one French critic labeled the pictures "fauves," or wild beasts. The name stuck.[2]

# The Starry Night

Throughout his life, Vincent van Gogh struggled with psychological issues and depression. In fact, Van Gogh painted *The Starry Night* in 1889 from the window of the asylum to which he had himself committed. The painting aptly mirrors his mental state at the time. Using his trademark bold brushstrokes and color, the painting does not necessarily depict the scene he saw but instead captures how he felt as he looked out the window. Van Gogh's work was some of the earliest expressionist art, through which artists express emotions instead of objectively representing forms.

He actually trained to be a preacher, but was fired and turned to art instead. Ultimately, he produced more than 1,000 works, many of which used a somewhat abstract style of bright color and bold brushstrokes he developed himself. Much of Van Gogh's work uses color to express emotions and communicate experiences.

Early on, Cézanne embraced impressionism and its use of vibrant colors. Yet his work was not widely recognized, and ultimately he pulled away from his colleagues. During this time, he developed his own style, which included building form with color and experimenting with subtle changes in tone. Cézanne's style developed through a series of still lifes. To create a sense of dimension in his work, he began using color gradations in each brushstroke, as opposed to contrasts of light and dark. His methodical study

## The Eiffel Tower

Just as the invention of new paints and portable easels transformed the way painters worked, new technologies and the use of steel transformed architecture during the late 1800s. At 984 feet (300 m), the Eiffel Tower was the tallest structure in the world at the time of its construction in 1889.[3] Its iron frame creates transparency, blurring the distinction between the interior and exterior of the tower. Designed by French civil engineer and architect Alexandre-Gustave Eiffel, the tower laid the foundation for completely new architectural designs in the 1900s.

At first considered an eyesore, the Eiffel Tower laid the foundation for completely new ideas in architectural design.

of the interplay of colors and patterns and how the eye perceives them is apparent in his landscapes, including such works as *Mont Sainte-Victoire* (1887). Cézanne's unique use of color laid the foundation for abstract art in the 1900s.

# Chapter 7

# Into the 1900s

$\mathcal{I}$n the Western world, the first half of the 1900s saw rapid social, political, and technological changes. It was a time of instability and seemingly out-of-control change. Reflecting these cultural changes, the art of that time period saw an increasing diversification in style, approach, and technique.

Artists at the time experimented more than ever before. Pieces were increasingly abstract, seeking to express emotions or ideas instead of creating a realistic picture. Other artists turned to the unconscious mind and their dreams as subject matter. And, overall, there was less regard for academic ideas of what art should be.

Edvard Munch's painting *The Scream* embodies the art movements of the early 1900s, which focused on expressing emotions.

Art changed more radically at this time than at any point in history, resulting in numerous new art movements.

# Expressionism

While the goal of the impressionists was to capture a moment in time, the aim of expressionist artists was to use shape and color to express emotions in nonnaturalistic forms. Though *The Scream* (1893) by Edvard Munch predated the expressionist movement, art historians often point to this painting as the embodiment of the movement's spirit. The painting depicts a primal scream from a distorted figure surrounded by dramatic colors. The work conveys strong feelings of terror.

The true origins of this movement are found in the works of Van Gogh and Matisse. One of the hallmarks of their style was the use of bolder, brighter colors than the impressionist artists. Expressionist art also moved away from realism and instead used distorted shapes and flat forms.

## THE UNCONSCIOUS

In large part due to the work of psychoanalyst Sigmund Freud in the early 1900s, people began exploring the notion of the unconscious mind. Freud described the unconscious as "a special region of the mind, shut off from the rest."[1] He believed people usually accessed the unconscious only through dreams. As Freud's work became more well known, artists began using the ideas and images of their dreams as a source of inspiration.

In his painting *Composition No. 6*, Wassily Kandinsky used bold colors, lines, and whirling forms to express the emotional power of music.

Another founding father of expressionism was Wassily Kandinsky. His work also laid the foundation for a growing interest in abstract art. In his series of ten paintings called *Compositions*, he sought to express the emotional power of music with paint. *Composition No. 6* (1913) is a combination of bold colors, lines, and whirling forms. To the untrained eye, the piece is entirely abstract and nearly impossible to interpret. However, Kandinsky composed the work with great attention to the focal points of the piece, the contrasting colors, and the types of lines applied. Paul Klee, a Swiss painter, also believed in the power of color to express emotions. As Kandinsky did, Klee used colors as musicians use instruments to evoke feelings. They believed the elements of art—color, line, form, and shape—could be used to evoke an emotional reaction.

# Cubism

A second new style emerged during the early 1900s from the work of Pablo Picasso and others. In 1907, this Spanish artist created an oil painting titled *Les Demoiselles d'Avignon*. It depicts five women using simplified features, distorted shapes, and sharp curves and angles. It is easy to see what Picasso meant the painting to depict, but it is not a naturalistic image by any means. Critics hated it at the time. But the French artist Georges Braque saw the work's potential. From that point on, Picasso and Braque worked together, conceiving new ways to represent what they saw and the purpose of art itself. They experimented with breaking up shapes and flattening a picture's space. After fragmenting an object or figure, the artists rearranged the parts to construct new images. Over time, their work became increasingly abstract.

The term *cubism* originated from a comment by an art critic who said these paintings looked as if they were made up of little cubes. The critic did not like this style, yet his description was actually quite apt, as cubist work is comprised of basic geometric shapes represented by blocks of color. Many people did not appreciate the extreme new ideas of Picasso and Braque, but others saw their work as the future of art.

## Dadaism

Following World War I (1914–1918), the Western world was disillusioned. The war had brought chaos, and civilian and military deaths numbered into the millions. People questioned how and why such mass destruction could have happened. In response, many artists revolted against everything that had led to the war. The Dada movement emerged in 1916 from this school of thought. These artists believed reasoning and logic had led

## Collage

The word *collage* comes from the French verb meaning "to glue." Collage artists use fragments of different materials of various sizes, shapes, textures, and colors to create an image. Beginning in 1912, Picasso and Braque first transformed collage into a serious artistic medium. They began by arranging cut pieces of paper to construct their cubist images. Ultimately, they began using media that made their collages three-dimensional.

to the horrors of the World War. Thus, Dadaistic art is characterized by the nonsensical and absurd.

In New York City, French-American artist Marcel Duchamp not only created an irreverent reproduction of the *Mona Lisa* but also began taking already made, ordinary objects and turning them into art. For example, in 1917 he took a porcelain urinal, placed it on its back, signed it with a fictitious name, and declared it to be a sculpture titled *Fountain*. The Society of Independent Artists summarily dismissed the piece for entry. Duchamp's choice to use a urinal as an artistic medium was intended to make the viewer think about what can be considered art. Duchamp himself believed merely the act of choosing the urinal gave it a new meaning.

## Surrealism

Beginning in 1924, the surrealist movement took Dadaism one step further. Surrealists such as Salvador Dali and René Magritte also spurned logic, reason, and reality. They focused their work on the unconscious mind, especially as revealed through dreams. The surrealists attempted to make visible the things people cannot see. The oil painting *The False Mirror* by Magritte represents many of these themes. The image is one of an eye, with the iris a blue sky dotted with puffy white clouds. This painting represents both the real world and a dream world and gives viewers the sense they are seeing and being seen at the same time.

While critics considered Magritte's *The False Mirror* to be representational surrealism, other surrealist work was more abstract. Much of the work of Spanish artist Joan Miró aptly represents this trend toward the abstract in surrealism. For example, his oil painting *Dutch Interior, I* (1928), combines an abstract assembly of bright colors, curving lines, and odd shapes. It creates a playful scene that also re-creates a 1600s painting in a new, nonrepresentational way.

## Frank Lloyd Wright

Just as artists were experimenting and innovating at the beginning of the 1900s, so too were architects. In the United States, Frank Lloyd Wright's architectural innovations included asymmetrical designs and structures that interacted with the environment. He specialized in homes, although he also designed the famed Guggenheim Museum in New York City. In the Midwest, Wright designed a series of homes dubbed the Prairie Houses. They were given this name because their horizontal, linear design seemed to echo the plains of that region. While not initially accepted, Wright ultimately gained international fame.

# Art in the United States

While artists in Europe were experimenting with increasingly abstract works, Americans were using art to establish national and regional identities. Their work often portrayed subjects that were recognizably American, including landscapes and rural or agricultural American life. This was happening during the 1930s, a time when America was struggling with the Dust Bowl, the Great Depression, and the country's position in the world, all of which also appear in the work of American artists.

Photographer Ansel Adams, known for his stunning black-and-white photographs of the American West, intended his work to inspire conservation and wilderness preservation in the United States.

Grant Wood's work depicts life in America's heartland. His most famous painting, *American Gothic* (1930), has become an iconic image in the United States. It portrays a stoic farmer and his prim daughter in front of their humble home. The image also suggests they are religious, hardworking, and conservative. While some

Critics disagree whether Grant Wood's iconic painting *American Gothic* was meant to mock or celebrate the farming lifestyle.

critics felt the painting mocked this lifestyle, most agreed it captures something profoundly American.

Another prominent American artist of the 1900s was Georgia O'Keeffe. While art historians consider her

## PHOTOGRAPHY

As with other American artists in the first half of the 1900s, American photographers captured images during this time that represented their view of the country. During the Great Depression, President Franklin Roosevelt created a series of programs commonly called the New Deal to decrease unemployment and help people through the tough economic times. The programs even funded artists, one of whom was photographer Dorothea Lange. Camera in hand, Lange documented rural and urban poverty in the United States. One photograph, *Migrant Mother, California,* taken in 1936, drew attention to the suffering of the poor. This image is credited with a rush of government assistance to migrant workers in California.

works to be abstract, she nonetheless remained independent from any of the rapidly shifting movements of her time. O'Keeffe built a reputation for representing elemental forms in nature with basic colors, shapes, light, and textures. O'Keeffe's hallmark images include colorful, bold close-ups of flowers, bleached animal bones, and the rugged southwest terrain.

The movements and styles of American art in the first half of the 1900s varied widely. Yet they had one thing in common. Twentieth century artists tended to care less about what critics thought and more about their own artistic expression of thoughts, emotions, and subjects as they perceived them.

# The Harlem Renaissance

Hundreds of thousands of African Americans relocated to the North to escape poverty and racism starting during World War I and continuing into the 1930s. During the Harlem Renaissance, a cultural and artistic movement lasting from 1917 to 1935 that flourished in urban areas in the Northeast and Midwest, African Americans continued struggling against racism and sought greater freedom.
But they also began developing distinctive culture and art. Jacob Lawrence was one of the leading visual artists of this movement. He was only 23 when he created his critically acclaimed *Migration Series* paintings, which depicted the lives of African Americans moving from the rural South to northern urban neighborhoods. Lawrence called his style "dynamic cubism," but the most powerful influences on his work were the shapes and colors of New York City's Harlem neighborhood itself.

# Chapter 8

# Post–World War II Art

*F*ollowing the devastation of World War II
(1939–1945) in Europe, the center of Western art
shifted to the United States for the first time. Set against
a backdrop of prosperity, expansion, and the developing
consumer culture in America, artists continued pushing
the limitations of traditional mediums, using new
materials and new techniques. Art evolved continually
after World War II, from increasingly abstract work
that explored the collective unconscious to the
use of everyday consumer items as art to creating
three-dimensional illusions on a flat surface.

The work of abstract expressionists such as Jackson Pollock invites closer inspection.

# Abstract Expressionism

The debate over what constitutes art also intensified after World War II, as artists began to experiment with using anything and everything to create their work. During the 1940s, the abstract expressionism movement took root in the United States, building on the themes explored in earlier abstract art.

Like the surrealists, the abstract expressionists used the unconscious as a subject. But rather than considering primarily the individual mind, they chose to explore the collective unconscious. This refers to the idea of memories, symbols, and feelings shared by all human beings. These artists were also heavily influenced by World War II, which had damaged human faith in science and logic, leaving many people feeling

## Assemblage

Assemblage is to sculpture what collage is to a flat surface. Artists use found objects and assemble them into a sculpture. This was a significant break from the traditional idea of sculptures carved from stone, wood, or other material. One of the first artists to experiment with assemblage was Picasso, who created his work *Guitar* in 1914 using pieces of sheet metal. Dada artist Duchamp also created assemblages, which he called "readymades," including his work *Fountain*. The term *assemblage* only became mainstream when a group of such works appeared in a 1961 exhibition called *The Art of Assemblage*.

life is uncontrollable. Artists at the time were concerned about the dark side of human nature. The abstract expressionists created much of their work on enormous canvases filled with color and abstract forms and focused on the physical act of painting.

Jackson Pollock, an American painter, exemplified this style. Pollock is known for his dripping and splattering of paint. His "action paintings" are measured in feet, sometimes as large as 8 feet by 17 feet (2.4 m by 5.2 m).[1] He worked on his paintings as they lay flat and moved around the canvas, painting from all sides. At first glance, his work may seem childish or uncontrolled. But the truth is, he exhibited great control to create his works. He varied the thickness of the paint, altered the pace and direction of his movements, and changed the sizes of the brushes or sticks he used. Pollock created his pictures as he

## PERFORMANCE ART

As art in the second half of the 1900s took on new forms, performance artists began experimenting with the idea of replacing stationary media with movement and sound. Artists performed these works before a live audience. Similar to their contemporaries, performance artists sought to move away from the constraints of traditional art. Starting during the late 1960s, such performances took place outdoors or in galleries, lasting from only a few minutes to a few days. One early example is the collaborative duo known as Gilbert and George, who referred to their works as living sculpture and performed across London, England, during the 1970s.

went, claiming to let his unconscious and intuition guide him. In his own words, "The painting has a life of its own. I try to let it come through."[2]

## Pop Art

Like others before them, pop artists mocked academic, classic art. They took everyday consumer items from popular culture and presented them in new ways as art. This movement began in the United Kingdom during the 1950s. By the 1960s, it had spread to the United States. Artists such as Andy Warhol and Roy Lichtenstein began using items from consumer culture as their subjects. One of Warhol's most famous creations, *Campbell's Soup Cans* (1962), features 32 different soup varieties. Each can is painted on a canvas 20 inches by 16 inches (50.8 cm by 40.6 cm).[3] These were installed evenly spaced on the wall of a

The work of Swiss psychologist Carl Jung promoted the idea of a collective unconscious and recognition of universal symbols. These ideas became central to artists' use of symbolism in both the surrealist and abstract expressionism movements.

Pop artists such as Andy Warhol (whose painting *Self Portrait* is shown here) mocked academic, classical art.

gallery in Los Angeles, just as cans on a supermarket shelf would be spaced. The work was a comment on the mass-production of consumer goods in the United States. Ultimately, Warhol even mass-produced his own work in a studio he named The Factory.

British op artist Bridget Riley attempted to disorient the viewer with many of her works, as with this painting, *Untitled (Circular Movement)*.

Assistants generated most of the work according to Warhol's specifications and guidance. Warhol then signed the finished products when they were complete. This method of creating art prompted further debate over what art is.

## Illusions

The op art movement continued challenging the definition of art. Short for "optical art," this new style emerged during the 1960s. Op artists including Bridget Riley sought to question simple truths about perception. They created the optical illusion of movement and depth on a flat surface using geometric shapes along with patterns of lines and colors. Similar to many other artists of this era, op artists did not create images to represent people, places, or objects, but instead tried to disorient the viewer.

Other artists of the time, including the well-known graphic artist M. C. Escher, were committed to experimenting with art and creating works that were not only creative but also intellectual. Many artists at this time believed the value of a piece is in the artist's idea, not in the work that stems from the idea. Artists working after World War II continued to push the limits of what art could be, do, and express.

## Minimalism

Is a dot in the center of a canvas art? What about a row of bricks stacked horizontally against each other on the floor? These works capture what is meant by the term *minimalist*. This style reduces art to its most basic forms without any attempt to create representational images or sculptures. These artists focus on simplicity and avoid any self-expression in their work. While some claim this is actually anti-art, the artists who produce minimalist works generally do so with the purpose of creating new forms instead of reusing old ones, rebuking traditional art.

# Chapter 9

# Contemporary Art

The contemporary time period began roughly around 1970 and includes artists who are still living and producing work today. Contemporary art cannot be classified by any one style but instead is characterized by many styles and media that reflect globalization and the enormous changes taking place in the world all around us. During this contemporary period, more than ever before, artists have been freer to express themselves in any form they can imagine.

## Art with a Message

The Western world has experienced great social upheaval over the past few decades. Contemporary

Contemporary artist Keith Haring's work often depicts social and political themes, as in this segment of a mural in Barcelona, Spain, which he created to protest against AIDS in 1989.

artists have been witness to the emergence of numerous social movements working to gain equality for all peoples, no matter their gender, race, or sexual orientation. At the same time artists from all backgrounds, including folk artists whose work was traditionally unappreciated or marginalized, moved into the mainstream. This combination of forces allowed artists to use their work to speak to the social upheaval and change in the world around them.

The push for civil rights began in the United States during the 1950s and gained momentum during the 1960s. African-American artists have used art to bring light to civil rights issues and racism, as well as to establish black culture and identity. In the United States, artist Faith Ringgold produced works that depict the truth behind racial prejudice and draw attention to the barriers facing all women. In 1983, she created a quilt titled *Who's Afraid of Aunt Jemima?*, which tells a story on pieced-together

## GLOBALIZATION

During the unprecedented growth of technology and communications at the beginning of the 1900s, the world seemed to become smaller. Telephones, cell phones, the Internet, and satellites have forever linked almost every corner of the globe instantaneously. This globalization has also eliminated cultural boundaries. The effect on the art world is that ideas spread more quickly than ever before. The influence for a work of art can now come from the farthest corners of the world.

squares of dyed and painted fabric. The story features a stereotypical black "mammy." Yet in Ringgold's work, Jemima is seen as a capable, strong businesswoman. Similarly, artist Chris Ofili uses his work, including *The Holy Virgin Mary*, to explore ethnic identity on a global scale.

In a similar manner, Mexican artists such as muralist Diego Rivera and painter Frida Kahlo used their art to illustrate the history of Mexico, Mexican culture, and the struggles of both the common and native

Mexican muralist Diego Rivera used his art to illustrate the history of Mexico, as in this mural located at the National Palace in Mexico City.

peoples. One of Rivera's best-known works, *Ancient Mexico* (completed in 1935), is displayed in the National Palace in Mexico City. It depicts scenes from his country's history, including native people struggling against Spanish colonizers.

In the second half of the 1900s, Native Americans also spoke up in the face of ongoing injustices. Artist Jaune Quick-to-See Smith grew up on a reservation in Montana. She knew she wanted to be an artist from the time she was a little girl. Her work reflects her self-identity as a Native American. She uses art as a platform for her beliefs, through which she can tell a story and get people's attention. Her masterpiece *Trade* (1992) is a monumental piece made from mixed media that features both abstract and collage elements. While the image of a canoe is central to the work, it also features newspaper clippings revealing the issues facing Native Americans living on reservations. Above the canoe hang both Native American artifacts and objects using the logos of contemporary sports teams with Native American names. There is also dripping red paint across the image, symbolizing the blood of Native Americans shed as settlers pushed them out of their homelands.

Among those also seeking civil rights were women. One of the best-known works to arise from the feminist movement was *The Dinner Party* (1979) by Judy Chicago. This installation piece was assembled between 1974 and 1979 by more than 400 women. The piece is a triangle measuring 48 feet (14.6 m) on each side featuring place settings honoring 39 women whose achievements were minimalized or left out of history books.[2] The women honored include artist Georgia O'Keeffe, poet Emily Dickinson, and even ancient goddesses. *The Dinner Party* projects a sense of community and a spiritual connection between women. Another female artist, Barbara

## Advertising

In the modern age of consumerism, it is no wonder companies use art to sell products. Art, after all, presents an idea or image oftentimes intended to evoke emotions. For centuries, art has been used as a form of propaganda. In today's consumer culture, art is used to persuade consumers to buy products. Today students even go to college to study advertising and design to learn how to best sell products in print, on television, and in the digital world. However, some argue that advertising is not art at all. The debate about the line between art and advertising, if there even is one, is ongoing.

Kruger, uses her work to undermine the ways in which the media reinforces gender stereotypes. Kruger was born in 1945 and is still creating art today. Her photo collages look like advertising posters or billboards. Using graphic design, she confronts the oppression of women and their bodies with slogans and images that challenge the onlooker to examine gender stereotypes.

The issue of gay rights came to a head during the AIDS epidemic of the 1980s. New York photographer Robert Mapplethorpe's images unsettled and challenged Americans and brought to light not only the subject of homosexuality but also the crisis of the AIDS epidemic. One body of his work, *The Perfect Moment*, included images of homosexual men as well as a series of self-portraits documenting how Mapplethorpe changed in appearance as his health declined due to AIDS. The show opened amid controversy in December 1988 in Philadelphia. Mapplethorpe died a few months later.

## New Media

Like other artists since the beginning of the 1900s, contemporary artists use an ever-increasing array of media for their work. Environmental art emerged during the 1960s. This movement refers not to art concerned with environmental issues, but art that uses the environment as its medium. Artists use a specific location to create a work such that the environment and the piece interact and the art becomes part of its location. For example, Colorado artist Michael Grab creates balanced rock sculptures in Boulder Creek. The rocks are simply balanced atop one another, with gravity as the only "glue" holding them together. Grab pays close attention to the shape and texture of each rock in order to create this balance. In the age of recycling, artists have also taken to using recycled and so-called "found" materials to create art.

# The Digital Age

No other invention in the history of the world has produced such rapid changes or offered so many possibilities for experimentation and innovation as the computer. Since its inception, artists have manipulated digital data to create art. This includes photography, drawing, design, and more. For artists, computer technology has unlimited potential that grows exponentially as technology advances further.

But while computers have changed how people create art, they have also revolutionized how people disseminate and interact with art. Since its "birthday" on January 1, 1983, the Internet has created powerful opportunities for artists to publicize their work. Online artists can share their creativity easily with an audience of millions across the globe. Many digital artists are less concerned with issues of ownership and copyright than artists in the past, and simply want their work available for the world to see. Artists can also use digital media to extend the life of a physical project. For example, following a physical show, the online community can remix images and video from the project to create something entirely new. In this way, computers allow art to evolve and take on a life of its own.

Perhaps the most powerful aspect of the digital age is that is has extended the possibilities of human creativity and imagination more than anyone ever dreamed. The world has been forced to redefine its ideas about artists, studios, and museums. There is no longer

Digital technology has pushed the boundaries of what is possible in art.

any preconceived idea of what can be created, and the answer to the question "What is art?" is as broad as the imagination of the human mind.

# TIMELINE

### 30,000 BCE
Human beings create some of the first cave paintings.

### 28,000–25,000 BCE
The *Venus of Willendorf* figurine is carved.

### 900 BCE–30 CE
Greek civilization and culture reaches its height, and the Parthenon is built in Athens around 440 BCE.

### 27 BCE–337 CE
The Roman Empire reaches its height, dominating three continents and creating further advancements in art and architecture, including the Pantheon (118 BCE–28 CE).

### 537
The Hagia Sophia, the largest church in the world for 1,000 years, is finished in the Byzantine Empire.

### 1100s–1500s
Art and architecture enter the Gothic period.

## ▪ 1150–1250

The Age of the Great Cathedrals includes the construction of the Gothic-style Cathedral of Notre Dame in the 1100s and 1200s.

## 1400–1600

Artists such as Leonardo da Vinci, Michelangelo, Donatello, and Jan Van Eyck reexamine and utilize the styles of the classical Greek and Roman artists and humanism during the Renaissance.

## 1600–1750

Art and architecture enters the baroque era, which includes the completion of the extravagant Palace of Versailles in 1685.

## 1750–1850

During this period of romanticism, artists focus on emotions and the imagination over reason and thought.

## 1840–1900

The artists of the realist movement depict real people going about their everyday lives. Claude Monet's work lays the foundation for impressionism.

# TIMELINE
# CONTINUED

### 1874–1886
Monet, Pierre-Auguste Renoir, Mary Cassatt, and other impressionist painters experiment with the interaction of light and color to capture the impression of a single moment in time.

### 1880s–1890s
Postimpressionists such as Vincent van Gogh, Paul Cézanne, and Paul Gauguin attempt to capture feeling through a more systematic use of line, form, and color.

### 1900–1935
Artists of the expressionist movement seek to portray emotional experiences and feelings in their artwork.

### 1907–1920
Pablo Picasso and Georges Braque initiate the cubist movement, rejecting naturalistic works in favor of shapes, distorted forms, fragmenting objects, and increasingly abstract work.

### 1916–1920
Dadaist artists reject authority in favor of absurdity and unpredictability.

### 1917–1935
The Harlem Renaissance explores the culture, heritage, and identity of African Americans in the United States.

### 1940–1960
Abstract expressionism emerges as the first major art movement in the United States.

### 1954–1974
The pop art movement reflects postwar prosperity and consumerism by using everyday objects as subject matter.

### 1960s
The works of op artists create the optical illusion of movement, disorienting the viewer.

### 1970–Present
The era of contemporary art emerges, involving a broad array of styles and media; it also includes art with a social message concerning the rights of African Americans, women, Native Americans, and homosexuals.

### 1980s–Present
The digital age changes how art is created, shared, and viewed.

# GLOSSARY

### classical
The high point of Greek and Roman art and architecture.

### commission
To order or request something to be made.

### contemporary
Beginning or occurring in the present or recent times.

## medieval

Of or relating to the Middle Ages, roughly the time in between the fall of the Roman Empire and the emergence of the Renaissance (400 to 1400 CE).

## secular

Not overtly or specifically religious.

# ADDITIONAL RESOURCES

## Selected Bibliography

Bird, Michael. *100 Ideas That Changed Art*. London: Lawrence King, 2012. Print.

Chilvers, Ian. *Art That Changed the World*. London: DK, 2013. Print.

Davies, Penelope J. E., et al. *Janson's Basic History of Western Art*. Boston, MA: Pearson, 2014. Print.

Kleiner, Fred S. *Gardner's Art Through the Ages: A Concise Global History, Third Edition*. Boston, MA: Wadsworth, 2011. Print.

## Further Readings

Barnet, Sylvan. *A Short Guide to Writing About Art (10th edition)*. Upper Saddle River, NJ: Pearson, 2010. Print.

Dillon, Patrick. *The Story of Buildings*. Somerville, MA: Candlewick, 2014. Print.

Mason, Antony. *A History of Western Art: From Prehistory to the 20th Century*. New York: Abrams, 2008. Print.

## Websites

To learn more about Essential Library of Cultural History, visit **booklinks.abdopublishing.com**. These links are routinely monitored and updated to provide the most current information available.

## Places to Visit

**Art Institute of Chicago**
111 South Michigan Avenue
Chicago, IL 60603
312-443-3600
http://www.artic.edu
This museum's permanent collection includes more than 300,000
works of art. Collections include Western art from ancient
civilizations to the present, as well as African, Asian, and Native
American works.

**The Museum of Modern Art (MoMA)**
11 West Fifty-Third Street
New York, NY 10019
212-708-9400
http://www.moma.org
The Museum of Modern Art in New York features modern and
contemporary artists using many different media. The museum
offers both permanent and traveling exhibitions, films, and
performances.

**Smithsonian American Art Museum**
Eighth and F Streets, NW
Washington, DC 20004
202-633-1000
http://www.americanart.si.edu
This museum displays a wide variety of artworks, chronicling both
the history of art in America as well as the American experience
from the colonial period to the present.

# SOURCE NOTES

## Chapter 1. What Is Art?

None.

## Chapter 2. Caves, Carvings, and Classics

1. Marilyn Stokstad. *ART-A Brief History*. Upper Saddle River, NJ: Pearson, 2004. Print. 33.

2. Fred S. Kleiner. *Gardner's Art Through the Ages: A Concise Global History, Third Edition*. Boston: Wadsworth, 2011. Print. 66.

3. Ibid.

4. Jerry Camarillo Dunn Jr. "The Pantheon." *How Stuff Works*. How Stuff Works, n.d. Web. 25 Aug. 2014.

5. John Kissick. *ART-Context and Criticism*. Madison, WI: Brown & Benchmark, 1993. Print. 90–93.

## Chapter 3. The Middle Ages

1. "Hagia Sophia." *Encyclopedia Britannica*. Encyclopedia Britannica, n.d. Web. 25 Aug. 2014.

2. Marilyn Stokstad. *ART-A Brief History*. Upper Saddle River, NJ: Pearson, 2004. Print. 172.

## Chapter 4. The Rebirth of Classical Ideas

1. Marilyn Stokstad. *ART-A Brief History*. Upper Saddle River, NJ: Pearson, 2004. Print. 281.

## Chapter 5. Moving Away from Classical Ideals

1. Penelope J. E. Davies, et al. *Janson's Basic History of Western Art*. Boston: Pearson, 2014. Print. 391–392.

2. Fred S. Kleiner. *Gardner's Art Through the Ages: A Concise Global History, Third Edition*. Boston: Wadsworth, 2011. Print. 318.

3. Penelope J. E. Davies, et al. *Janson's Basic History of Western Art*. Boston: Pearson, 2014. Print. 431, 439–440.

# SOURCE NOTES CONTINUED

### Chapter 6. Impressionism and Beyond

1. Fred S. Kleiner. *Gardner's Art Through the Ages: A Concise Global History, Third Edition*. Boston: Wadsworth, Cengage Learning, 2011. Print. 370, 588.

2. Penelope J. E. Davies, et al. *Janson's Basic History of Western Art*. Boston: Pearson Education, Inc., 2014. 552–553.

3. "Eiffel Tower Facts." *Science Kids*. Science Kids, n.d. Web. 25 Aug. 2014.

### Chapter 7. Into the 1900s

1. Gertrudis Van De Vijver and Filip Geerardyn. *The Pre-Psychoanalytic Writings of Sigmund Freud*. London: Karnac, 2002. Print. 133.

## Chapter 8. Post–World War II Art

1. Penelope J. E. Davies, et al. *Janson's Basic History of Western Art*. Boston: Pearson, 2014. Print. 602.

2. Ian Chilvers, chief consultant. *Art That Changed the World*. London: DK, 2013. Print. 356.

3. Penelope J. E. Davies, et al. *Janson's Basic History of Western Art*. Boston: Pearson, 2014. Print. 610.

## Chapter 9. Contemporary Art

1. "Henry Thoreau Quotes." *Henry David Thoreau Online.* Thoreau-online, n.d. Web. 25 Aug. 2014.

2. "The Dinner Party." *Judy Chicago*. Judy Chicago & Donald Woodman, n.d. Web. 25 Aug. 2014.

3. Penelope J. E. Davies, et al. *Janson's Basic History of Western Art*. Boston: Pearson, 2014. Print. 632–633.

# INDEX

# ABOUT THE AUTHOR

Laura Perdew is a former middle school teacher turned author. She writes fiction and nonfiction for children, including numerous titles for the education market. She is also the author of *Kids on the Move! Colorado*, a guide to traveling through Colorado with children. Laura lives and plays in Boulder with her husband and twin boys.